Also by Donald Revell

Collections of Poetry

Tantivy, Alice James Books, 2012
The Bitter Withy, Alice James Books, 2009
A Thief of Strings, Alice James Books, 2007
Pennyweight Windows: New & Selected Poems,
Alice James Books, 2005
My Mojave, Alice James Books, 2003
Arcady, Wesleyan University Press, 2002
There Are Three, Wesleyan University Press, 1998
Beautiful Shirt, Wesleyan University Press, 1994
Erasures, Wesleyan University Press, 1992
New Dark Ages, Wesleyan University Press, 1990
The Gaza of Winter, University of Georgia Press, 1988
From the Abandoned Cities, Harper & Row, 1983

Prose

The Art of Attention: A Poet's Eye, Graywolf Press, 2007
Invisible Green: Selected Prose, Omnidawn Publishing, 2005

Translations

Songs without Words, by Paul Verlaine, Omnidawn Publishing, 2013
Last Verses, by Jules Laforgue, Omnidawn Publishing, 2011
The Illuminations, by Arthur Rimbaud, Omnidawn Publishing, 2009
A Season in Hell, by Arthur Rimbaud, Omnidawn Publishing, 2007
The Self-Dismembered Man: Selected Later Poems of
Guillaume Apollinaire, Wesleyan University Press, 2004
Alcools: Poems of Guillaume Apollinaire, Wesleyan University Press, 1995

Essay

A Critical Memoir

Essay

A Critical Memoir

Donald Revell

OMNIDAWN PUBLISHING
RICHMOND, CALIFORNIA
2015

Cover Art: *Beatrice Addressing Dante from the Car*
from *Illustrations to Dante's 'Divine Comedy,'* 1824–27
Pen and ink and watercolor on paper. Dimensions 372 x 527 mm.
Artist: William Blake 1757–1827
© Tate, London

Cover typeface: Kabel LT Std.
Interior Typefaces: Trajan Pro and Adobe Jenson Pro

Book cover and interior design by Ken Keegan

Each Omnidawn author participates fully in the design of his or her
book, choosing cover art and approving cover and interior design.
Omnidawn strives to create books that align with each author's vision.

Offset printed in the United States
by Edwards Brothers Malloy, Ann Arbor, Michigan
On 55# Heritage Book Cream
Acid Free Archival Quality Recycled Paper
with Rainbow FSC Certified Colored End Papers

Library of Congress Cataloging-in-Publication Data

Revell, Donald, 1954-
Essay : a critical memoir / Donald Revell.
    pages cm
ISBN 978-1-63243-001-4 (pbk. : alk. paper)
1. Poetry. 2. Poetics. I. Title.
PN1031.R47 2015
808.1--dc23

                                        2014040742

Published by Omnidawn Publishing, Richmond, California
www.omnidawn.com   (510) 237-5472   (800) 792-4957
10 9 8 7 6 5 4 3 2
ISBN: 978-1-63243-001-4

He must, without a miracle, become the perfection he has seen.

—Charles Williams

AS IT BEGINS, we are bold to say. Voluptuaries notwithstanding, we are bold to say. And so the very beginning steals ahead of me. I must fall in love. Immediately, a very great difference sets foot upon a stone bridge. *The Prelude* (1805), lovingly, is addressed to one particular friend, while *Leaves of Grass* (deathbed edition 1892) speaks to none but everybody, even to everybody, born and unborn, bold to say. Who's crazy? Whose pomp is prophetic? As neither Wordsworth nor Whitman ever set eyes upon Beatrice Portinari, I am stolen far ahead already, a breezy changeling. The Higher Criticism rocks an empty cradle, a redundant energy vexing its own creation. Out of a baby's fist: perdition. Out of Perdita's song and dance, the prophetic transaction. I can answer now. Wordsworth is the prophet, Whitman the crazy man.

HEAVEN NOTWITHSTANDING, but rather abandoning itself to the narrow stone bridge, I must hasten to add that Whitman is a madman only as an asymptote is mad. I must fall in love. A girl has already begun to make her way—in a progress, in a procession of one—towards the keystone from her farther shore. At this moment, I begin to number the heavens. Wordsworth ought to have done the same. We must remember: if he is a prophet, he is one of many. Therefore, the asymptote is mad. The curve of my eye can never touch the stride, the hem, the state of such as She, my beloved. The curve of the bridge falls short, into painted water and bitter isolation. (The poet Hart Crane, bless him, bless him, could never take his eyes away. For the very last instance of impeccable—i.e. innocent—close-reading, see Robert Creeley's letters to Charles Olson on the subject of Hart Crane: "Dammit/isn't that gentle!") Mad as the asymptote must always be, it is no fool. Beloved touches my eyeball and it burns. There is

11

a strange meeting above the keystone of the bridge. Born meets unborn, in illustrious transaction, and neither is a changeling anymore. Walt Whitman never wrote a poem, that's true. No voluptuary, but the bed-buggiest man God ever sent down from Heaven walking. Afoot with vision means: America is a prophecy without its prophet. Meanwhile, the new pageant cradles a viol, miming Love, LOVE, as Chaplin spoke the darling word in silent pictures, in aftertimes.

ALBION IS SICK; America faints! etc., etc., mimes the music and the wordlessness. The Pageant of Amor is rapture from beginning to end, Heaven's slow, ceremonial, irrevocable transaction. Even costumed as a childhood ragbag Balthazar, a king at last after so many Christmas Eves a shepherd, St. Peter's Church Westchester Avenue annual pageant, I could not spoil the silence. I turned to the other kings. Pointing to the manger, I shouted "He's here! He's over here!" No one heard, and no one afterwards remembered anything amiss. This is the use of memory and precisely how it came about that an American boy, schooled by English nuns in the shadow of the elevated subway #6 Pelham Bay Park to Brooklyn Bridge said "Whitman" meaning "Blake," said "Chaplin" meaning "Crane" in the very last car of the airborne passing train. How can one joy absorb another when each joy is a Love? America faints. Beatrice Portinari has stepped upon the keystone of a narrow bridge, an asymptote touching the curve of an infant's eye or perdurable tiny fist. W.H. Auden, I believe, was one of the loneliest men in the world. I am thinking not so much of his biography—the solitude of an always more-loving genius, his dying alone in his sleep in a hotel bed in Vienna—as of the endless appeal to communion and to companionship in the conversation of his work. In the end, Echo remained a stranger at the altar rail, and Narcissus the uninvited guest in his every caesura. Consider this passage from "The Poet and the City."

> Originality no longer means a slight modification of one's
> immediate predecessors; it means a capacity to find in any work

of any date or place a clue to finding one's authentic voice. The burden of choice and selection is put squarely upon the shoulders of each individual poet and it is a heavy one.

WEEP I CANNOT, but my heart bleeds. Albion is sick. From such a crowded, unstill, originary paradise of eidetic memory, what liberation? And yet, strangely enough, in the equal perfections of his kittenish isolations, T.S. Eliot broke free. (In Paradise, remember to tell Hart Crane Tom Eliot was his kitten in the wilderness; the fact that Tom grew up into three white leopards is neither here nor there. That Bohemia should be an island crowded with magical shepherds is neither here nor there. Canons are funny that way.) This is the chase!

> The emotion of art is impersonal. And the poet cannot reach this impersonality without surrendering himself wholly to the work to be done. And he is not likely to know what is to be done unless he lives in what is not merely the present, but the present moment of the past, unless he is conscious, not of what is dead, but of what is already living.
> ("Tradition and the Individual Talent")

After the parents' praise, after the ice cream, after the nuns had disappeared into the undercroft, kings and shepherds were free to speak, and the wordlessness of the newborn Child, and of his Love, absorbed them, absolved them. No one heard, and no one afterwards remembered anything amiss. This is the use of memory and precisely how W.H. Auden's loneliness, "a sort of *sanctus, sanctus, sanctus*," might effortlessly, in the kittenish mind and subway isolation, prophesy one and only one American poet, William Blake. "Oh, no, no! I see an innumerable company of the heavenly host crying 'Holy, holy, holy is the Lord God Almighty!' I question not my corporeal or vegetative eye any more than I would question a window concerning a sight." Voluptuaries notwithstanding, I fell in love.

Not in entire forgetfulness,
And not in utter nakedness,
But trailing clouds of glory do we come
From God, who is our home…

THIS, I KNOW, is not from *The Prelude* but, rather, from
"Ode: Intimations of Immortality." An identical truth, even only
unequivocal, shines throughout the poetry of Thomas Traherne.

Into this Eden so divine and fair,
So wide and bright, I come His son and heir.
("The Salutation")

From the nineteenth century to the seventeenth, and so on and on,
we might easily work our way backwards to the original syllable
at the very first moment of creation. All works instantly obviated
by the Work, there'd be no poems then. (It happened to Rimbaud.
Having witnessed, in the unequivocal, undistinguishing bliss of
his declarative, "Christmas on earth," he had nothing more to say.)
All of our conversation and poetry, every cradle we distinguish
from another, exists by grace of a fine distinction: "Not in *entire*
forgetfulness;" "not in *utter* nakedness." That a fine distinction
might ultimately be fictional is a determination reserved to the
moment of death, and we're not there yet. For now, the least
memory, the most threadbare garment, scripts a beautiful pageant.
Among its countless attributes, a pageant is the interval between
vision and prophecy. It is virtually wordless, but it transforms,
it changes *utterly* the visionary Word. As it happens, we call the
transformations Poetry. Walt Whitman never wrote a poem. Once
in Paumanok, he came upon a nest, and he just couldn't contain
himself. Somebody heard, and someone afterwards remembered
everything amiss.

I BEGIN TO NUMBER THE HEAVENS. It is something like
counting, beginning from God, who is our home. Certainly, this is

14

as much to say that June 8 of the year 1290 remains very far ahead, in a distance without bridges or one in which the bridges have all been raised, abandoned by the bridge-keepers. To say "beginning from," as does Wordsworth, as do you and I when the ice cream has been finished and the Pageant of Amor undertaken out of costume, places heavy emphasis upon that awful word *from*. Any number afterwards aches with loneliness. Such numbers pressed very harshly upon Auden, and he would not ignore them or debase their forward fact. There's no going backwards to beatitude. Whitman counted up the eggs in the nest. Voluptuaries notwithstanding, voluptuousness is the land to which we go. Every work of every date or place already nestles, already mansions there. Trust Eliot to have set the mansions dancing, in sacramental conjunction, signifying matrimony. Trust is the only cure for loneliness that I know. Snow had fallen, and on the snow-clad steps of St. Peter's Church, in the minutes of midnight Christmas Eve, we waited for an elevated train to pass. We watched the empty sky above the ironwork. We listened in the empty silence left behind by steeple bells. When the Brooklyn Bridge-Pelham Bay local came, we aimed our snowballs into the opened doors between the cars. The game was to hit anyone seated just inside. Any one.

> Slater, let me come home.
> The letters have proved insufficient.
> The mind cannot hang to them as it could
> to the words.
>
> There are ways beyond
> what I have here to work with,
> what my head cannot push to any kind
> of conclusion.
> (Robert Creeley, "Hart Crane")

The game meant simply counting up to one, if anyone could ever count so high, if anyone's aim and arm strength were up to it. The solitary man just inside the car could never be Hart Crane. He was drowned, washed far away where Lycid lay. It might, however, be his good friend Slater Brown. But no. In the Christmas of which I'm thinking, he was away to the north, dreaming of lemon squares and hot coffee in the morning in Gloucester, Massachusetts, just the other side of the island from his home in Rockport. Robert Creeley told me so in 1987 in Denver, when Slater was still very much alive. And so we three kings and several shepherds never counted to one, not really…though I remain to this day sorry for any man we sometimes managed really to hit. He'd be staring straight ahead into a black bell-tower streaking past. And then the snowball. "Slater, let me come home," but there's no going back. Beatitude's dark backward and abysm, even when its proper name is God, presses hard and presses forward.

(I MUST AT THIS MOMENT INTERVENE, interject, interleaf…if either you or I should die before the voluptuaries disappear entirely into their countless beatitudes—one and by one and one, footfalls on a narrow bridge—it will be the death of Allegory of which we died. I could at this moment walk away into the open pages of *The Romance of the Rose* and onto a patch of grass, Fort Tryon Park, 1970, boys hurling themselves towards the battlements laughing, girls laughing in the spotless, vertical midair above the fray. Allegory is safekeeping. Happiness exists under its actual name, independent of boys and of girls. Who could live without it?)

PRESSING AGAIN FORWARD NOW—to the battlements, boys!—beginning from God, it is something like counting. Cling to the simile if you will, but remember also that simile is the smaller lens. Eternity widens at the other end of the telescope, onto the prospect of Allegory, which is our home. Once in Paumanok

> When the lilac-scent was in the air and Fifth-month grass was
> growing,
> Up this seashore in some briers,
> Two feather'd guests from Alabama, two together,

And their nest, and four light-green eggs spotted with brown...
("Out of the Cradle Endlessly Rocking")

AND EXACTLY HERE IS WHERE WHITMAN sees
his poem fly away from him, if seeing has anything true to say,
anything *like* a black bell-tower and then snow. He couldn't contain
himself. The numbers came and came on. Multitudes cannot walk
the narrow bridge, nor even half so far as Alabama. Multitude is
mothering, and mothers fly away home. Press hard, press forward,
laughing all the time, and the girls in middle air move the stones
beneath your feet. It is something like counting, but without
numbers. The mind cannot hang on to them. Beatrice is pendant to
Beatrice farther on, just as Happiness is pendant to itself. Atta boy!
Atta boy!

> Time is but the stream I go a-fishing in. I drink at it; but while I
> drink I see the sandy bottom and detect how shallow it is. Its thin
> current slides away, but eternity remains. I would drink deeper;
> fish in the sky, whose bottom is pebbly with stars. I cannot count
> one. I know not the first letter of the alphabet. I have always been
> regretting that I was not as wise as the day I was born.
> (*Walden*, "Where I Lived, and What I Lived for")

Thoreau is bold to say. And even to say is to adventure the risk
of counting without numbers, to accept the infant (but not the
forgetful, not the naked) disadvantage of writing without an
alphabet in mind. At Walden Pond, and everywhere that *Walden*
goes, Time is a pageant of eternity. Had Whitman never counted
months or eggs, perhaps a pageant rather than an asymptote of
wayward *thanatos* might have come to Paumanok. If, instead of
"The word final, superior to all," he had managed somehow a strong
and delicious wordlessness to say...Solecism is the grammar of
Allegory, only archaic in the dark backwards and abysms. Prophecy
chooses its prophets, not the other way around. Trailing clouds
of glory, the wise child remains effectively invisible quite a while.
"He's here! He's over here!" is the cry nobody but the voluptuary

newborn Jesus hears when nothing is amiss. Childe Roland takes a snowball in the face.

IT GOES FAST, as Robert Creeley was fond of saying. Eternity remains. A pageant continues in prophetic leisure. Wordlessness drinks deeper and goes fishing in the sky. Under its actual name, Happiness is the story that continues by beginning. A little pomp, if you please, and a breezy changeling setting out on a festival day (nothing like Whitman's otherwise gorgeous "outsetting bard") sees a Beatrice bound for glory.

IT SLOWS DOWN. At Walden Pond, the ceremony of innocence never drowned. The ceremonial transactions—stars for a pebble, heavens for earth—memorialized a patch of ground that, in good time, became a book. It's the ceremonies that make time good and make of memory itself a living companionship. Of course I'm thinking of a girl, but I am thinking too of countless companions: Chaplin knocking on Hart Crane's dizzy door; angels coming to Auden's hotel bedroom; magical shepherds crowding an island in Bohemia.

REBIRTH IS NOTHING as compared to being born again. In pageantry, there is always recurrence, but never, not even when the same ridiculous, scruffy boy plays Shepherd #2 for the umpteenth year in a row, is anything made to happen again. Jesus hated to repeat himself. (Hence his anger with Satan in the wilderness, and hence the cruel accuracy of his prediction to Peter concerning cock-crow.) We'll never get anywhere, you and I, until we share the sense of "born again" as absolutely and perfectly unprecedented, because it never happened before. After all, no one heard me shouting in St. Peter's Church, and no one remembered anything amiss. It was Christmas.

BETTER TO COME TO YOUR SENSES head-over-heels by a stream near Walden Pond than to suffer rebirth. Better to discover flowers by lore than by number. Ophelia beside a stream in Elsinore. Matilda beside the rivers of the Earthly Paradise. Perdita disguised as Perdita at the sheep-shearing. Not by rebirth but by being born again do we get ourselves to the show. We go the pageant expressly to be born again, and again, always faring farther on, voluptuaries notwithstanding. Better to be abandoned on the landlocked oceanfront of imaginary Bohemia than to be devoured by bears.

> …Blossom, speed thee well.
> There lie, and there thy character: there these,
> Which may, if fortune please, both breed thee, pretty,
> And still rest thine. The storm begins. Poor wretch,
> That for thy mother's fault are thus exposed
> To loss and what may follow! Weep I cannot,
> But my heart bleeds. And most accursed am I
> To be by an oath enjoined to this. Farewell!
> The day frowns more and more: thou'rt like to have
> A lullaby too rough. I never saw
> The heavens so dim by day. A savage clamor!
> Well may I get aboard. This is the chase!
> I am gone forever.
> > *Exit, pursued by a bear*
> *[Enter a Shepherd]*
> ("The Winter's Tale," III.3 ll. 49-61)

Perdita becomes Perdita abandoned, being born again as herself entirely elsewhere. There's no going back. Antigonus, her deliverer, never makes it back to the ship that carried them away from imagined adultery. Perdita's conception *becomes* immaculate. Discovered by the shepherd, the princess is born again as a shepherdess to become, in the fullness of time, and thanks to the longest scene in any of Shakespeare's plays, a Queen in Bohemia. Perdita never repeats herself. She recurs and recurs, a foundling in the pageant, with a new crown still to come. *Incipit vita nova.*

BEING A LIFE, the new life has its passages—from danger to rescue, from beasts and abandonment to shepherded festal days. They become cosmic sometimes: Dante awakens from a dream of Beatrice to eternal Beatrice, finding himself harried in a dark wood by three fierce creatures. Then off he goes across the universe. The passages are sometime fierce in durable privacy, compassing inward hours and events "that do often lie too deep for tears." But there are always flowers. Eventual hymning rose, dooryard lilac, down to "the meanest flower that blows:" prophecy and allegory, the human urge to transport and every means of transportation are transacted best in flowers. Love is our interval. Its currency is colors, textures, scents, and names. Love is the time spent learning to fall in love with Time. Marvell had it right. The pageant of ourselves "Does through a fragrant zodiac run." The asymptote of Art touches a curve of Nature, calling names but, really, calling flowers. Where you or I might play at pastoral, eternity plays for keeps. Perdita never repeats herself.

> ...Here's flowers for you:
> Hot lavender, mints, savory, marjoram,
> The marigold, that goes to bed wi'th'sun
> And with him rises weeping...
> ....Daffodils,
> That come before the swallow dares, and take
> The winds of March with beauty: violets, dim,
> But sweeter than the lids of Juno's eyes
> Or Cytherea's breath: pale primroses
> That die unmarried, ere they can behold
> Bright Phoebus in his strength—a malady
> Most incident to maids: bold oxlips and
> The crown imperial: lilies of all kinds,
> The flower-de-luce being one.
> (IV. 4 ll. 120-122, 136-145)

FLOWERS ARE ONCE AND ONCE ONLY. In pastoral, in pageantry, they recur and recur; but here, even in Shakespeare's most capacious and unruly scene of true mistaken identities, each is seen to be said only once. Art imagines a line while Nature bends towards Paradise. Flowers are faster than their names. Stars speed out of our constellations. Bridges cross us. What was Whitman counting? Could Dante ever have counted the days beyond June 8? Things flourish in the direction of the countless; art flourishes towards wordlessness. As King Polixenes, disguised as a shepherd, says to the shepherdess Perdita, unknown even to herself as a future Queen: "over that art,/Which you say adds to nature, is an art/That nature makes." Back in the Bronx, Shepherd #2 was a loud King coming on.

AS SHEPHERD #2 COMES, perhaps for the last time, once again into view, I ask his question: Is beauty, when it occurs as an accident of substance—the last minute child, the dime store (there were dime stores then, the "Five & Tens" as we called them) naked baby doll promoted Messiah—any the less beautiful, any the less substantial for being accidental?

NATURE BENDS, and it is easy to discount the wordless before and the wordless afterward of her glimmering arc. We experience our intervals of beauty and of love so deeply, so *extensively*, that we commonly relegate pageant, pastoral and allegory to unlettered dumb-shows or to quaint imaginations of the afterlife. Yet, in bending, Nature encloses. Our intervals, however truly deep, however extensive, are chords and radii, asymptotes made true by Nature's way. The pageant is true. The dime store naked baby doll is real. Messiah is real. A name, a Jesus if you will, passes between them on a glimmering arc. The Pageant of Amor is, as Polixenes says to Perdita, "an art/That nature makes."

WHATEVER COMES NEXT, it is always, thank Heaven, a masque of *Walden* improvised momently, a pebbly heaven and star-strewn riverbed. The sky is a bow, the river an arrow. The bow is Arjuna's and the river is Amor's. A rainbow for Noah, a shower of golden rain arrowing down on Danae. It goes on and on, but never to be counted. The Maypole accountancy of allegory and the *dramatis personae* of pageantry, since before the very first pageant began, admit of no numbers but assume innumerable names. Hence Arjuna. Hence Amor. And hence *You know me, Al.* (Alpha, Aleph, Hester Prynne a few miles to the east of Walden Pond.) The straight line upon which Nature bends towards Paradise is imagined by you and Dante, me and Perdita, and the ladybird who flew away from Paumanok and from her mate. That brings us to Beatrice. She is not imaginary. The absolutely perfect curve of her smile echoing the curve of a bridge in Florence is reality projected *by* reality all the way home. The projection is the pageant. I am turning it up a notch, and far beyond a snowball's throw. The pageant of Beatrice unfolds at the brink of Heaven. Voluptuaries be upstanding!

I FELL IN LOVE. Whether I shall turn out to be the hero of my own life, or whether that station will be held by anybody else, these pages must show. Question a window concerning a sight, and always the same answer: I fell in love. Question the pageantry, and always the answer is a boy's own name, changed a little, *la revestita voce alleluiando.* Afterwards, "Beatrice Addressing Dante" by William Blake featured beautifully in color on the cover of *The Norton Anthology of Poetry* over many years, including many I am minding now, miming LOVE, which yet must have had a long foreground somewhere, for such a start.

BETWEEN SOMEWHERE, actually an anywhere I call Beatitude, and the beginning—A, the beginning of Amor, a few miles east of Walden Pond—lies the brink of Heaven. There are thresholds in every direction and, as the asymptote said to the archangel, Heaven lies on the other side of each. It lugs us back lifeward, bone by infant bone, as Hart Crane said to the stripper. Shall these bones live? Crossing thresholds, we lose the distinction between words and wordlessness. The loss is the being born. The loss is a given name. *Dante, perche Virgilio se ne vada,/non pianger anco, non piangere ancora,* the only time in the *Commedia* that

22

Dante's name is written down. Beatrice says it; Dante faithfully writes it down, her very first word in a very long time. Still, the gaps in eternity are hardly any time at all. Just enough for the pageant—in this case, Cantos XXIX and XXX of *Purgatorio*. And subsequently, in Blake's colors, and on the cover of my durable anthology, covering the years of my loves.

{*Aside*—On a murphy-bed, 1974, in Johnson City, New York, reciting poems of Robert Lowell to someone reciting poems of Robert Creeley.

> Poor ghost, old love, speak
> With your old voice
> Of flaming insight
> That kept us awake all night.
> (Lowell, "The Old Flame")

Of course Beatrice, *l'antica fiamma*, is never poor, nor ever ghost, nor old.

> Let me stumble into
> not the confession but
> the obsession I begin with
> now. For you...
> (Creeley, "For Love")

Of course Dante never confesses to any obsession beyond one girl's given name.}

BEATITUDE AND VOLUPTAS hold us together. Allegory holds us all together, keeps the thresholds in vivid motion and close contact. One is the threshold Wordsworth strews with clouds of glory. One *could* have been—Walt Whitman never wrote a poem—Paumanok's gray beach swathed in whispers. Each is a brink of Heaven on the brink of saying. "He's here! He's over here!" No one hears, and no one, if he is paying such close attention that mere accounting never comes to mind, remembers anything amiss. At the very end of *A Week on the Concord and Merrimack Rivers* (written on the shore of Walden Pond—we mustn't forget that *Walden* is a book about writing the book prior to itself): "It were vain for me to endeavor to interrupt the Silence." Nothing amiss describes precisely and extensively the space of a pageant. Before too long, something like conversion comes around, "for poetry has more in common with worship than with philosophy or theology" (Helen Gardner, *The Art of T.S. Eliot*, 61). Beatitude and Voluptas hold us together without a doctrine. Allegory holds us together without dogma. It is the pageant we *become*, when first the pageant speaks a name, our name, that makes the asymptote come around right. It bends into worship, not pushing on forever to endless unrequital (one Vienna hotel bed after another), but arcing, curving as an eye or as a keystone curves, along the arc of conversion. The old flame, the flower-de-luce, the naked dime store baby doll promoted Messiah, turn our loves towards home. Objects such as these comprise what Charles Williams, in *The Figure of Beatrice*, calls "the breathing heraldry of fact." These bones live. We have brothers (e.g. my three brothers, dead before I was born) and sisters, say an eight years child at the Florentine Maypole, in Elysium with beloved toys for us, turning us.

> To Christian and non-Christian conversion is incomprehensible. (Gardner 104)

BREATHING HERALDS COLOR the stillness and the extravagant, actual décor preceding our names. Another word for "décor" is Nature. The extravagance, for Christian and non-Christian alike, refers actually to God—the created universe is nothing if not an extravagance. The heralds "Teach us to care and not to care" ("Ash Wednesday"). And after the stillness comes a turning, an incomprehensible yet somehow comprehensive arc of couples paired before and after the pageantry—Beatrice and Dante, Perdita and Florizel, Miranda and Ferdinand, Marina and…well, T.S. Eliot addresses Marina perfectly and for all time. Before means

Beatitude. After means Voluptas. The incomprehensible middle is
Amor.

The pageant leads to a turning.

> Yet mot I need amenden in some wyse,
> Right through the vertu of your heigh servyse.
> (*Troilus and Criseyde*, Book 3, ll. 1287-88)

Amenden colors the motion green, according to *vertu*, the motive.
Heigh indicates direction, *servyse* a way to go. The unprecedented
homecomings up ahead remember nothing short of Love. After
the stillness comes a turning, the arc of couples. "We must be still
and still moving/Into another intensity" ("East Coker"). Anything
else would be literally unimaginable. (Exactly here would be the
place to insert one's own Theory of the Imagination.) The upturn
never looks back to see the asymptote it was. Innocence can afford
to be extravagant, not counting the cost. Don't ask Orpheus. Ask
Eurydice.

I KNOW THAT THERE ARE ATHEISTS, but I cannot for
the life of me find them, not even one. Everywhere I turn I find
that my eyes find blessed couples. As Auden avowed at the zenith
of his lonely but irrefrangible Vision: "the blessed will not care
what angle they are regarded from,/Having nothing to hide" ("In
Praise of Limestone"). Into this carelessness disappear all questions
of translation. Words and wordlessness: one and the same. Pomp
and prophecy: one and the same. The shout of a boy dressed up as
Balthazar was never anything amiss. Shepherds and kings: one and
the same. Let us count what *can* be counted.

> It is required
> You do awake your faith. Then all stand still.
> On: those that think it is unlawful business
> I am about, let them depart.
> ("The Winter's Tale," V.3 ll. 114-117)

25

OUT OF PAGEANT, still and still moving, the couples lawfully depart—upward according to the arc provided, the pattern of their loves. Beatrice and Dante proceed through Earthly Paradise, past chariot and griffin and newly flowering trees. Their better Eden is scarcely the beginning of Heaven. Perdita and Florizel, pastoral shepherdess and shepherd no more, leave their imaginary Bohemia to witness the real magic. In instantaneous pageant, the statue of Hermione comes to life. Innocence triumphs in every direction, and better marriages, and more immaculate conceptions, are still to come.

> Music; awake her: strike!
> 'Tis time: descend: be stone no more: approach:
> Strike all that look upon with marvel.
> ("The Winter's Tale," V.3 ll. 120-122)

For Miranda and Ferdinand, just one Shakespearean comedy farther on, Prospero's nuptial pageant ("Now come, my Ariel! Bring a corollary,/Rather than want a spirit: appear and pertly./ No tongue! All eyes!") melts "into air, into thin air." Words and wordlessness plight their troth in Allegory. Reverie ends, and the rightful Duke of Milan is portrayed by the rightful Duke of Milan himself. Such is the loving Nature (pearls and eyes testify to the extravagance of Creation) of Allegory. Such is the realism of Allegory.

Dear Walt: the low delicious word is Love.

Scholium

ALLEGORY IS A PAGEANT of metaphor and simile. Trailing clouds of glory all its own, figurative language comes upon the scenes of our imagining there. No poet writing in English writes pageantry so in-close as does Robert Herrick. Here, in its entirety, is "The Coming of Good Luck:"

> So Good-luck came, and on my roof did light,
> Like noiseless snow; or as the dew of night:
> Not all at once, but gently, as the trees
> Are, by the sunbeams, tickled by degrees.

Given substance, shape, and agency, Good-luck enters upon the advent of itself. Notice how it remains itself—not embodied by snow, not portrayed by snow, but given over to a like behavior, a noiselessness. In pageant, then, there are two: Good-luck and snow. Then there are three. "The dew of night" adds to noiseless Space (the snowy rooftop) the quiet Time of night. Given space and time, then, Good-luck is wholly born.

ONCE BORN, Good-luck possesses not only similitude, but absolute Being. The enjambment between lines three and four is climacteric. "As the trees" leads us to expect another simile; but suddenly, capitalized and alone, stands the one word "Are." Snow and night and trees all blend into plural singularity, into the apotheosis of Good-luck. Apt to apotheosis, there is radiance; Herrick provides "sunbeams." Here, "Are" is the instance of Amor, after which the upturn bends, "tickled by degrees" towards home. After the radiance, we are returned to homely simile: "as the trees are tickled by degrees." But with this difference: an apotheosis added, embedded. Herrick's figures of speech alone could not have anticipated such a birth.

OUT OF ALLEGORY they emerge, the words and phrases, into pageants great and small. They return home afterwards, completing a world in which allegory and fact, allegory and actual experience, are one flesh.

> Ek gret effect men write in place lite;
> Th'entente is al, and nat the lettres space.
> (*Troilus and Criseyde*, Book 5, ll. 1629-30)

> …The storm of flung flowers rises and falls, and in that cloud of beauty 'donna m'apparve—a lady appeared to me…She wore some kind of dress 'di fiamma viva—of living flame', and over it a green mantle; white-veiled, olive-crowned, she paused there, and Dante—
> The great pageant has been so, and more than so. We may not be able to stay its pace, but Dante could. He has heaped up references and allusions; he has involved doctrine and history and myth, and the central dogma of the twy-natured Christ itself. He has concentrated meanings, and now the living figure for whom all the structure was meant is here.
> (Charles Williams, *The Figure of Beatrice*, 178-179)

Reverie is at an end. Purgatory might well have been a pilgrim fantasy, and Inferno a gothic nightmare. Dream visions sort very well with vengeance and remorse; they are the pretty conscience of child's play. But Paradise, upon whose brink the breathing heralds of Allegory welcome Beatrice, is real. Beatrice speaks a name: "Dante." And Dante writes it down. Allegory is splendid entertainment, but it entertains neither mask nor alias. Dante crosses over. Heir of allusion and son of reference, he crosses over into pageant and Paradise under his given name. He's wide awake—*Voi vigilate ne l'eterno die.* The story is true. William Blake has painted so many eyes into the picture. There are witnesses.

IT'S NO ACCIDENT that upon the verge of Heaven itself, Dante hesitates for eight full cantos. He is all eyes. He is the pageant while the pageant lasts. In *Purgatorio*, earthly paradise is Eden still, regained through material witness. In states of perfection, all things are exculpatory evidence of themselves. I want to cross over under my own names, all of them, alongside pageantry. Yet it's not by accident that I hesitate. I like my allegories allegorical. "Better...to stay cowering in the early lessons, since the promise of learning/Is a delusion," as John Ashbery writes ("Soonest Mended") so early and so well. Allegory is safekeeping. It is shield and buckler in the mock-siege of spring 1970, Fort Tryon Park, New York. Boys hurl themselves towards the battlements. Girls, laughing in midair in false miniver, urge them on. Simply to remember them, as one amongst them, is to know that Happiness exists: Allegory the shield; Allegory the buckler; Allegory the actual Name, walking away into *The Romance of the Rose*. Together in eternity now, the authors appear, historically, in ideal sequence. First, Guillaume de Loris, poet of the opening 4,000 lines. His story is true. Happiness is the image of itself. How do I find it?

> ...by keeping steadily before you both the literal and allegorical
> sense and not treating the one as a mere means to the other but
> as its imaginative interpretation; by testing for yourself how far
> the concept really informs the image and how far the image really
> lends poetic life to the concept.
> (C.S. Lewis, *The Allegory of Love*, 157)

FORT TRYON PARK WAS EDEN STILL. I was a boy. I was there, part and parcel of the tatty materials, and I bear witness to it still. It's there to be learned forever in the first 4,000 lines or so.

> ...few poets have struck better than Guillaume de Lorris the
> note which is the peculiar charm of medieval love poetry—that
> boy-like blending (or so it seems) of innocence and sensuousness
> which could make us believe for a moment that paradise had never
> been lost.
> (Lewis 169)

MOMENTS HAVE A WAY of yielding to the next moment—
"some climbing/before the take-off," as Ezra said, speaking also
of battlements and Paradise and of voluptuaries turning upwards
out of pageant, continuing the pageantry. Guillaume de Lorris,
poet of courtly love, yields to Jean de Meun, poet, scholar, sceptic,
and tireless exegete. Adding 19,000 lines of his own, completing
The Romance, de Meun takes the Rose by storm, by sheer force of
numbers.

> It was the misfortune of Jean de Meun to have read and
> remembered everything; and nothing that he remembered could
> be kept out of his poem.
> (Lewis 188)

I think that we all, one way and another, become the Jean de
Meuns of ourselves. We annotate the finest days again and again.
We exhaust our happiness, meaning only to complete the dream.
We lay broad waking. The only cure for love, Guillaume, is to love
more. As for de Meun, as for ourselves in the long afterglow of the
great poems, we must read more. We must travel the allegory the
right way round.

COMMITTED TO THE SAFEKEEPING of every name,
commodius vicus brings a traveler the right way round. Back from
the brink leads back to the brink and also to questions of conduct.
What is a fallen man to do in Eden when Eden never fell? Love
more. Read more. William Blake painted many eyes into the
picture. A man could use them. As a through passenger—

> My head is hands and feet. I feel all my best faculties concentrated
> in it. My instinct tells me that my head is an organ for burrowing,
> as some creatures use their snouts and fore-paws, and with it I
> would mine and burrow my way through these hills.
> (*Walden*, "Where I Lived, and What I Lived for")

As a tourist—

…you would be so thoroughly prepared to understand what you saw—You would make fewer traveller's mistakes.
(Thoreau's *Journal*, June 12, 1851)

As prodigal son—

Life is not long enough for one success.
(*Journal*, July 19, 1851)

Return excels itself by virtue of a simple turn. Sing the Shaker hymn. Sing it with Henry.

Here or nowhere is our heaven.
(*A Week on the Concord and Merrimack Rivers*, "Friday")

Is Grasmere just across the verge of Paradise? Does a man, on the far side of pageant, forgive the fathering child he was? Is Paumanok Eden? Is the absconded she-bird forgiven, either by her fathering mate or by the out-setting bard? Loving more, reading more, the painted eyes begin to number the heavens. Is England a green and pleasant one? Is America?

Walt, tell me, Walt Whitman, if infinity
Be still the same as when you walked the beach
Near Paumanok—
(Hart Crane, "Cape Hatteras")

Brink and verge and selvage: crossing over, up, and into the pageant, close-reading is close-loving. "My hand/in yours,/Walt Whitman--/so—." My head is hands and feet: all eyes.

SO VERY CLOSE is first a cloud of emblems, images, words. So very close—loving reading, reading loving—the qualities of joy are indistinguishable from objects each possesses. My cloud was on the cover of *The Norton Anthology of Poetry*, in color. "Beatrice Addressing Dante" by William Blake shows an awakening cloud, envisioned as colors blazoned forth with eyes in plumage, eyes in flowers, pageant-wise.

cosi dentro una nuvola di fiori
che de la mani angeliche saliva
e ricadeva in giu dentro e di fiori,

sovra candido vel cinta d'uliva
donna m'apparve…
(*Purgatorio* XXX 28-32)

All the loves at once, *donna m'apparve*, a lady appeared to me—says Dante, says I, says anyone whose name is spoken aloud on the skirt of Heaven. It's written down. In the spring of 1972, in Professor G's Introduction to Literary Analysis, and on a narrow bridge through flowers and farther, into the mounted policemen surrounding the Pentagon, all the loves at once appeared, *una nuvola di fiori*, already written down. I fell in love a dozen times. "Beatrice Addressing Dante" was a cloud I carried everywhere it carried me. Numbering heavens, 1972 was such a number, each numeral possessed by joy.

How can one joy absorb another? Are not different joys
Holy, eternal, infinite! And each joy is a love.
(*Visions of the Daughters of Albion* 124-125)

The daughters of 1972 appeared to me as gaze in plumage, gaze in flowers, asymptotes of actually beautiful human *being* touching the curve of my eye. Said curve continues pageant now, for joy. And Blake was right of course. One joy cannot absorb another. Eyes do not absorb the light. They rise to it, pageant-wise. I'm saying nothing about symbols. This is allegory. My college, Harpur College, was then, as now, incorporate with Binghamton University. The school itself, however, was not *in* the city of Binghamton. More heavily wooded then than now, campus lay to the west, in the town of Vestal. I lived very near, on Vestal Avenue, number 123, upstairs. It was a four-room apartment, to begin with. Sometime in March, one of the rooms came away and fell into the street. The monthly rent remained the same. My weekly writing assignments for Professor G likewise remained the same: 500 words on "Among School Children." Yeats' pages in my *Norton* were the heavily annotated skirt of the cloud I carried everywhere, and a long schoolroom too. I am sixty this year, smiling. As I was smiling in 1972 when Professor G invited me to dinner and I saw, for the one and only time, her remarkable daughter. I've forgotten her name. She wore a cream-colored dress with intricate bodice. Her only jewelry was a crucifix, silver, set with five red stones. All the air and all the light of that evening belonged to her. She spoke very little. She smiled often. I have never forgotten. There was pretty plumage once. This is the chase! (From among the heaped-up references and allusions, it is proper to choose from "The Winter's Tale;" in the fall of '72 I would take Professor G's Shakespeare class, and there would come a morning when, staring out a window into the small, first snow, listening to her sing to us a song of Autolycus', I was born. There was a mischievous breath between small snow and William Shakespeare I had never breathed before. My life ever since depends upon it.) The daughter's smile and unaffected elegance, the color of her cheek and hair, made her a daughter of the swan to my close-reading eye. In "Among School Children," Yeats names no woman's name, but she goes without saying. "Ledaean" suffices. In pursuit of atonement, not of possession, close-reading is chaste. In the spring of 1972, I loved them all and was lover to none. Atonement is magical chastity: "a living child"; "yolk and white of the one shell." Sylvia, an Arcadian by name, was the friend of some friends of mine. One afternoon I saw her fall and tear the seat of her dungarees. The gesture, the nonchalance (to use Whitman's word) with which she folded the rough tear together and went on speaking to her friends, was unspeakably lovely. I'm saying nothing about symbols. This is allegory. I fell in love, and never spoke to her until an accident of the anti-war movement made a change. In Vietnam, the Easter Offensive— which dragged on well into the autumn—was horrifically underway. Protests and escalations kept steady pace with atrocity on all sides, in all dialects and distortions. Not a single branch or trellis flowered that April and May, in Vestal, in *echt* Binghamton, in Syracuse (where a strange girl kissed me the softest kiss of my life as a policeman took away my whistle and my flag), in Washington DC (where I saw *Sesame Street* for the very first time with two small girls who called me "Mr. Demonstrator" because I was a guest in their parents' home), and across the river in Northern Virginia (where many ran a gauntlet of bowing branches and rearing horses, I with those same two children under my arms, to escape the tear gas), but that branch or that trellis seemed outraged or afraid. It's hard to smile when all that smile are terrified, even the flowers and small girls. No one is comfortable, and no one lives to grow old beneath a gauntlet. I had my *Norton* with me everywhere. I continued writing my weekly assignments "Among School Children" literally, young and old, at play in peril. In the midst of all, "bent/Above a sinking fire" one late night on Vigil on a courthouse lawn, I spoke with Sylvia and got to know her, if only a little. Our purpose was solemn presence, round the clock, every day, in quiet protest of the arraignments and convictions of schoolmates subsequent to their arrest at other, more clamorous demonstrations around town. The midnight was damp and chilly; we were a drab contingent huddled around the fire I'd built in a trash barrel. (The police didn't mind. This was Binghamton, New York, a gentle place. In the morning, they'd bring us buns and coffee.) Drab, except for Sylvia. After 40 hours' vigil, we'd looked to be the sullen, bewildered children we mostly were. For once, the heckler's daylight shout of "dirty hippies" would ring true. But not of Sylvia. Hers was a Ledaean body sure enough, and a face always tilted slightly across the shadow-line where, if you looked closely, a smile began. When she stepped into the circle of firelight, I stood up straight and tried my best to look like a Moses in fatigues, prophetic behind my skimpy beard. She was so nice, so easy in her zeal. She hated the War. She hated the draft. Everyone did, and so we might as well stay close to the fire and talk about music and school and summer plans. There was a long night still ahead. And so we talked, leaning into the warmth together, sometimes laughing. One by one, our companions drifted off to doze on benches, strum guitars, read beneath streetlamps. For a while, Sylvia and I were alone. Then, out of the shadows came a voice, and a man, not much older than ourselves, dressed in a business suit, stood beside us. He asked about the Vigil. In the long small talk, he got around to asking if a little break—a hot shower, forty winks in a clean, warm bed—sounded good to us. I must admit that I'd already thought of such things; but a room had only lately fallen away from my apartment on Vestal, and it would offer no refreshment to beautiful Sylvia. The stranger, in town on business, said he'd been given a suite by mistake at the Ramada, and we were welcome to the extra bed and bath if we liked. We liked, bewildered children as we mostly were. Suffice it to say that, back at the Ramada, we found our stranger's nature to be "but a spume that plays." Sylvia and I showered (separately of course). It felt good. And then we were indeed welcome to use the big, clean bed…provided that our host could, well, watch. Watch what? Sylvia and I ran back to the courthouse lawn, hand in hand. When the sun came up, policemen brought hot coffee and sticky buns. The morning had a festal air, a sunshine purpose with no war in sight. I never saw Sylvia again after that morning. Over the summer, she must have transferred to another school. In my weekly essay, I wondered about that man in the business suit, and what his "mother would think her son, did she but see that shape" squatting beside an empty, unruffled motel bed. All loves at once can sometimes come to naught. But I was among the blessed schoolchildren, studying pageant from the inside, according to the curriculum of pageant—"reading, writing, and flaming arithmetic" (John Ashbery, "And You Know"). I could number the heaven, one by one. *Donna m'apparve.* I counted by William Blake's four cardinal numbers for Daughters of Albion: one; holy; eternal; infinite. *Una nuvola di fiori* was everywhere in the spring of 1972, and out of every cloud of those days a Lady appeared to me. Reina was with me, on all roads, and I with her. My eyes in the yearbook photograph look towards Reina, behind the camera. She was in my kitchen making tea when a bedroom fell away into the Vestal

35

Avenue traffic. She wasn't frightened. She still came round to visit me nearly every day or night. She typed my papers for Professor G's Introduction to Literary Analysis. She steadied the horses at the Pentagon and made chaplets for herself and for two small girls from broken branches. She was not my lover, though my friends assumed she was, and I was proud to let them. She had an air so absolutely unique to herself, so *acceptable*—by which I mean to say that her mere presence made all things welcome, calm, accepting, unfailingly candid. Wherever she stood in her cloud of flowers, she was the flowers, even drifting into mind or midair. This is not symbolism. This is allegory. Goodness appears as herself, in the role of Goodness, and afterwards as a great deal more, though I know nothing about it. The "self-born mockers of man's enterprise" move too fast. I write poems, etc. The Easter Offensive gorged itself all summer and ended just before Christmas. Soon it was somebody else's war. By then, Reina had found a lover. Once, I saw her dancing with him at a concert in the Student Union, February 1973. There is such a thing as Hell. "How can we know the dancer from the dance?" Only by dancing. *Donna m'apparve* just to say that Youth and Beauty are one and the same, a Heaven secured by pageant evermore, if only. "Guardaci ben! Ben son, ben son Beatrice."

HESITATION AND DELAY must never be mistaken for rest. "Let us cross over the river and rest under the shade of the trees"— Stonewall Jackson's dying words. Rest is the efflorescence of right action: i.e. the Pageant itself. The brink, the near shore, the selvages, these are places of clamor. Rooms fall away. Branches fall away. No one afterwards remembers anything amiss. The spring of 1972 was one heaven to cross, in the direction of Heaven. (Asymptote hardly knows itself until—*Guardaci ben!*) 1973 was bound to come and bound to go beneath the chariot wheels of Youth and Beauty. "*Ben son, ben son Beatrice.*" Yeats, in the closing lines of "Among School Children," resigns himself to a frantic question. "How can we know the dancer from the dance?" But simultaneities are not identities. If they were, symbols would suffice. Allegory leads us quite a dance, but the dancing is real. The role of Love is danced by Love, and "each joy is a love." The symbolist eventually runs short of numbers. Allegory goes on. Even Wordsworth, who knew better, having voiced a perfect summa of pageant early in his Intimations Ode— "The Soul that rises with us, our life's Star,/Hath had elsewhere its setting"—runs short of breath and numbers by the end, resigning himself, like Yeats, to a conundrum: "Thoughts that do often lie too deep for tears." Hell is deep. Heaven is wide. The true measure, the true account of any motion is the motion itself.

> …Does his eye behold the beam that brings
> Expansion to the eye of pity? Or will he bind himself
> Beside the ox to thy hard furrow?
>
> ....
>
> Arise and drink your bliss, for everything that lives is holy!
> (*Visions of the Daughters of Albion*, 215-217, 223)

Albion is sick. There's no resigning. Light itself is motion touching human eyes. Position, heal thyself. "Position is where you/put it" says Robert Creeley ("The Window"). Beatrice says "*Guardaci ben!*" and suddenly Heaven is wider still. Blake at the very brink, where the brink *is* Heaven underway. One pageant is one success. Is there a life of mine in there, an America? I'm asking.

IN THE WORDS of an old Blues standard, "can I get to you now, Lord, or must I hesitate?" Perhaps it is Dante's delay and not his devotion I emulate. Am I afraid to cross over the river without my Virgil—my allusions, my heralds and cross-references? I must read more. Am I afraid to die? I must love more. *L'antica fiamma*, my old flame, is not old. In Heaven, Yeats, excess of love is not bewildered. On Heaven's brink, more is better. I must read more lovingly, until reading crosses over to rest beneath the shade of words.

STONEWALL JACKSON must have known which river to cross and exactly where, exactly when. Upon the brink of Heaven, so close, precision as to moment, precision as to place, is critical.

> …So, while the light fails
> On a winter's afternoon, in a secluded chapel
> History is now and England.
> (T.S. Eliot, "Little Gidding" ll. 235-237)

Only an American, most especially a Missourian, could have written those lines as pageant and not palaver. At the brink of Heaven, if you get it wrong, angelic hands cast no flowers—*una nuvola di fiori/che de la mani angeliche saliva*. Mermaids do not sing. There is an instance of upturn not to be missed. Our lives are loves, surely. But comes a time we must love rightly. Else we risk the oblivion of love, disappearing back to Limbo. Surely our loves appear in perfect order, in poetry, in pageant. Comes a time we must read rightly. Else we risk the oblivion of metaphor, disappearing back into the anthologies.

> Lovely enchanting language, sugar-cane,
> Honey of roses, whither wilt thou fly?
> (George Herbert, "The Forerunners" ll. 19-20)

In the crisis of mortality, Herbert urge his poetry to turn away from metaphor towards perfection. He urges Allegory. He commends the perfection of death-in-love reading the pageant of his own conversion, voluptuaries notwithstanding. Conversion is that instance of upturn *in* love, *in* Amor, inside of which loving and reading play a single part. For an instant (it ought to last forever) Pageant knows itself. Small wonder then, at the end of his writing life, Shakespeare should write "The Winter's Tale" and "The Tempest," tragedies of misreading that, via pageantry on islands, become comedies of redemption from oblivion and metaphor, of love restored to perfections more perfect than before.

IN "THE WINTER'S TALE," place and time escape the action of the play until returned by spectacle. Leontes, king of Sicilia, the true island home of pastoral poetry, of Theocritus and Bion, vexes his kingdom to nightmare with jealous, murderous misreading.

Courteous words are misread as adulteries. Reading fails. Love fails. Innocents die in prison. Unreality rules. A spotless newborn, Perdita, is abandoned on the nonexistent shore of Shakespeare's imaginary Bohemia. Only when Time itself, embodied pageant-wise in Chorus, speaks sixteen years of hallucinatory discord, does the healing festival begin. Florizel, a prince disguised as a shepherd, recognizes nobility in the now-grown foundling shepherdess Perdita. Pastoral turns towards home in tender Pastoral transaction. (Love perfects Courtesy; Courtesy perfects Love.) In pageant, *to* pageant, Pastoral returns to real Sicilia. There, the statue of the falsely convicted Queen Hermione comes to life, escaping oblivion, escaping metaphor, and all may read the truth of sweet reunion. Because of Love, reunion accomplishes more than the sum of its parts. Paradise is more than Paradise Regained. In pageant and allegory, the role of Love is always and only played by Love itself. Perfection shows ever more perfectly in the twinned originals.

IN "THE TEMPEST," the pageant of Amor rescues not only the shipwrecked, but rescue itself. Come to its appointed moment, Prospero's magic makes a difference but, for all its mischief and music, no real change. His book must drown before he can read aright. The lovers must tear "the baseless fabric" of his enchantments; only then do they love face to face. We may smile when Miranda, first seeing Ferdinand, declares "I might call him/A thing divine," and smile once again when later, in her final speech, she exclaims "How beauteous mankind is! O brave new world,/ That has such people in't." But she's not wrong. Nor is Prospero right in his bitter rejoinder, "'Tis new to thee." Love *is* divine in its beatific origins and voluptuous destination, and love makes all things new. There are several pageants within "The Tempest"; Ariel sees to that. But the play, in its valedictory entirety, is one great Pageant. Prospero misreads until he reads a book greater than his own. *That* book is sweet reunion. Miranda misreads until she no longer portrays an imago. Only *then* is she born, into the allegory of real life. Unmistaken love is fitted to fly. As Prospero avows:

There sir, stop:
Let us not burden our remembrances with
A heaviness that's gone.
(V.1 ll. 224-226)

In love, countless perfections are exchanged, lover to lover. They pass between us. This is the story, and the story is true. Just before she died, my sister took down a picture I'd cut from a magazine and kept on my bedroom wall. She had it beautifully, expensively framed, and hung it back on its crooked nail, without a word. It's a picture of Heaven—something medieval, a patch of garden in which the Blessed Souls exchange small tokens hand to hand, under the approving gaze of two angels and two deer. Perfections are equal in essence, but there is a hierarchy too. Cockermouth ("Much favour'd in my birthplace" says *The Prelude*), Paumanok, Eden, these are heavens of the original sort: beatific. Trailing clouds of glory, to each an asymptote of his own, we go the transit of loves. We play the pageant. Sometimes Shepherd #2 becomes a King. Kids are equal in essence, but somewhere in the lovely transactions of Amor, actually *inside* the transactions, happens an upturn and hierarchy. After the shepherd's festival, Perdita is not simply restored to Sicilia; she will be Queen there, and Queen of Bohemia too. After enchanted island exile, Miranda is not only restored to the duchy of Milan; she will be Queen of Naples, by and by. There are footsteps upon a Florentine bridge to consider also: *donna m'apparve*. Clouds are exchanged for crowns; heavens of the eventual sort (the event is Love) are Paradise, unjacketed and voluptuous.

IN OUR REAL LIVES, actual events are inseparable, one from another. Each is a passage from a single text: the pageant in which, eventually, we play all parts but one. To read more closely is to love more closely. And if, as near to the Beloved as we can say, words seem to fail, they have not failed. All structuralists are charlatans. "He's here! He's over here!" *Donna m'apparve*. Sometimes, we live

40

and have our being entirely *inside* the words. Loving so closely, our eyes read into the stars inside of eyes.

> The works of the great poets have never yet been read by mankind, for only the great poets can read them. They have only been read as the multitude read the stars, at most astrologically, not astronomically.
> (*Walden*, "Reading")

Which is simply to say that poems and stars exist. Greatness consists in the originals. Oothoon, in *Visions of the Daughters of Albion*, knows how to read. She can never be defiled or distracted, and her perfection (which is astronomical) improves with every word.

> How can one joy absorb another? Are not different joys
> Holy, eternal, infinite! And each joy is a love.

It is very tender to know that Oothoon will travel, like Perdita, like Miranda, all the way from cloud to crown.

> There is a grain of sand in Lambeth that Satan cannot find,
> Nor can his watch-fiends find it; 'tis translucent and has many
>   angles.
> But he who finds it will find Oothoon's palace, for within,
> Opening into Beulah, every angle is a lovely heaven.
> (*Jerusalem*, II ll. 383-386)

Loves remain distinct in their numberless heavens, each one in place, which is One place, never afterwards amiss. Which is to say that poems and stars exist and, further, to say "the stars are caught and hived in the sun's ray." That was Hart Crane speaking, his last completed poem, "The Broken Tower," speaking the most intense of Amor's deep transactions, inside of which perfection turns for home along a ray of sunlight. Staring straight ahead into a black bell-tower streaking past, the eyebeam touches the curve of the human eye, descrying Paradise. "Slater, let me come home." That was Robert Creeley speaking, in the role of Hart Crane in the singular pageant. And home they went.

Scholium

ON MY TABLE HERE I have a compact paperback (1966 Anchor Edition) of Hart Crane's poems and selected prose. It's my favorite, the last one published while New Critics ruled the earth and poems were safe to find friends of their own, and to keep them close for as long as friendship lasted. The book is built for intimacy. Here are poems that Frank O'Hara cherished at the very same hour in a very different Manhattan from that in which Robert Lowell likewise cherished them. These are poems Robert Creeley, in the most beautiful letters he ever wrote, taught Charles Olson how to love, while Allen Tate, a drinking buddy to Crane and to Slater Brown, was yet alive and writing well in his entirely different America. (There's a letter to Tate in this little book…"We're all unconscious evolutionists, I suppose.")

THIS IS NOT MY ORIGINAL COPY; it is a recent gift from a thoughtful graduate student. Thank you, Joseph, for, in your own words, "filling a gap." My original was left behind on an airplane circa 1989 en route to the MLA Convention in Washington DC. It was already a broke-back and yellowing item; I'd carried it with me on every sort of trip for a dozen years and more. Why? All for the sake of one stanza.

> And so it was I entered the broken world
> To trace the visionary company of love, its voice
> An instant in the wind (I know not whither hurled)
> But not for long to hold each desperate choice.

Here, in one lyric instant, are all the transactions of Amor perfectly, unguardedly compacted. The newborn seeks and finds a company, a pageantry. The way of affirmation, the visual, touches the *via negativa* upon auditory, imageless rhymes. Freedom of choice is a foundling awaiting the next instant, which must somehow, anyhow reveal image and voice imparadised.

Certainly, over the years there'd been a sense of increment. For a long time, it was only the phrases "broken world" and "visionary company" I loved and, imperfectly, grasped. Mishap and happiness, crisis and rescue—more than enough transit and transport for me. Still, over time it was the calm, the stateliness behind the (in)famous ecstasies of the poem that mattered more and more. The ups and downs, the gatherings and dispatch, the shattering diapasons, are not chaos. There is no delirium. Rather, Crane compacts a turbulence of transactions, all of them loving, into a single instance: "the stars are caught and hived in the sun's ray." Follow that ray to its source. There is no regression. Asymptote touches bell curve on the rise. Intimations all prove accurate. Origin is newly destined:

> And builds, within, a tower that is not stone
> (Not stone can jacket heaven)—but slip
> Of pebbles—visible wings of silence sown
> In azure circles, widening as they dip…

Uplift, "visible wings of silence," fits the affirmation of images like wings onto the auditory imagination. A compact is sealed into pageantry: "The commodious, tall decorum of that sky/Unseals her earth, and lifts love in its shower."

AS ONE OF THE EPIGRAPHS to *Four Quartets*, his crowning pageant of instances, T.S. Eliot chose this passage from Heraclitus: "the way up and the way down are one and the same." As the instantaneous epitaph to a life's work, "The Broken Tower" ends in a shower of lights raining up through clamor ringing down. No gaps.

> I must pass beyond memory to find you, my true Good, my sure Sweetness. But where will the search lead me? Where am I to find you? If I find you beyond my memory, it means that I have no memory of you. How, then, am I to find you, if I have no memory of you? (Saint Augustine, *Confessions* X 17)

FROM CLOUD TO CROWN, what becomes of memory is what comes of it. A secluded chapel for Eliot, a palace for Oothoon, azures for Crane, a brave new world for Prospero's Miranda, each of these is a voluptuary instance of voices and imagery imparadised, just as they'd been from the beginning, only now aware. It happens often, which is to say all the time When. The pageant cannot remember itself, and then it does. Saint Augustine's pilgrim anxiety finds a passage from resolution ("I must pass beyond") to something *far* beyond independence. Still, resolution drifts. It drifts a very long way, into "blank misgivings" as Wordsworth called them, into Dante's *selva oscura* where allegory ravens after messes of shadow meat. Sometimes it drifts all the way, as in Whitman, and eventually "the low and delicious word" becomes the death-in-life of "me." Allegory grows cold this side of Paradise. Vision that misses the upturn, the fording-place, the skirt of Heaven, *una nuvola di fiori*, never prophesies. Grace is a more-than-marvelous gift, but so is grit.

> out of all this beauty something must come
> (Ezra Pound, "Canto LXXXIV")

Pound's insistence acts on faith, and faith acts—radiance without let-up all through *Rock-Drill*. By grace or grit, perfection finds the turn for home inside of love, close-reading deep transactions written there. Close-reading prophesies. Prophecy is what becomes of memory, precise as to moment and to place.

AUGUSTINE PLEADS a further concern, as it is the very *substance* of memory—its *essential* Goodness and *essential* Sweetness—he cannot bear to relinquish. There's nothing to fear. In becoming prophetic, memory relinquishes nothing at all. The voluptuary instance changes everything, forsaking not one thing, not even the shadow or petal or skirt of one. Inside of Love, memory no longer passes, however tenderly, between subject and object. Passages are reunion. Reading is closer than grammar comprehends. Augustine will know the conjugations of his memory forever changed. Conjugal infinitives, as it were, cross over from Eden to Paradise, bringing the entire Garden home. It isn't a pageant for nothing. *Confessions* commemorates a God more sweet and good than even His saint remembered. Likewise, towards the end of *Purgatorio*, Virgil, hitherto Dante's unperfected memory of the Vision, disappears. He is not gone. He has become the dimensionless point exactly where Beatrice lowers her eyes, lifting the *Commedia* into Prophecy.

> Nothing matters but the quality
> of the affection—
> in the end—that has carved the trace in the mind
> dove sta memoria
> (Ezra Pound, "Canto LXXVI")

Dove sta memoria…where memory liveth. Having taken the upturn, having forded the river, having joined with metaphor in pageant where metaphor is purely itself, memory is a mere agency no longer. It is entity. The God whom Augustine so loved can neither be forgotten nor remembered. God lives, which is to say that all the Goodness and Sweetness dear to the saint freely live and freely act, *dove sta memoria*. As entity, memory fulfills the now prophetic pageant. Prophetic all along, it had merely been confused

46

with grammars. Entity is transit, not transitive. In *Confessions*, Augustine's love of God is perfected, revealed to have been in fact, and from before the beginning, God. In the *Commedia*, Dante's love for Beatrice transits an identical dimensionlessness, the eighth day of June 1290 notwithstanding. Reproof, and then a smile distinguish the Beloved in poetry, where memory liveth. *That* is why "Dante" appears just once in all the hundred cantos; his spoken name is a summons to prophecy, to actual entity. Only then is it written down.

THE VISIONARY WRITES no poetry, only regressions and reprise. Reproof (say that of Beatrice) and a name (say "Dante" written into *Purgatorio*) are tenderly required. I could mention a voice calling "Child" at the end of George Herbert's "The Collar." Or Robert Creeley en route to his own real name in "Heroes"—"That was the Cumaean Sybil speaking./This is Robert Creeley, and Virgil…" And then the asymptote curves into a smile, which is also the curve of a human eye, descrying Paradise. You can't make these things up out of thin air, or out of abandoned nests, or out of blown roses. No one believes you.

> That she is living,
> Were it be told you, should be hooted at,
> Like an old tale. But it appears she lives,
> Though yet she speak not. Mark a little while.—
> (*to Perdita*) Please you to interpose, fair madam. Kneel
> And pray your mother's blessing.—(*to Hermione*) Turn,
>   good lady,
> Our Perdita is found.
> ("The Winter's Tale," V.3 ll. 140-146)

Hermione alive is the mother Perdita never knew and therefore never had occasion to remember. To Hermione, Perdita is no foundling, but a daughter born full-grown in perfect love. Where memory liveth, memory is an altogether new adventure, an entity among other entities, where neither subject nor object appertains.

Imparadised, what Pound calls "the quality/of the affection" is a quality no more, not subordinate to humours and nuance. It lives free. Saint Augustine had nothing to fear. His memory lay always just ahead of him, where Goodness is entity and Sweetness is entity. The pageant of Amor answers to each part with all speed.

> Lead us from hence, where we may leisurely
> Each one demand, and answer to his part
> Performed in this wide gap of time since first
> We were dissevered. Hastily, lead away.   (*Exeunt*)
> ("The Winter's Tale," V.3 ll. 180-183)

WHAT BECOMES OF MEMORY is what comes of it. The very first photograph taken of my sister Roberta in Heaven dates from 1948. The cast of the St. Peter's Church annual Christmas pageant gather in full costume—a pastorale underneath balloons and mistletoe in the parish hall. The pageant has ended. You can almost hear a late train grinding through the midnight air outside and above. My sister, innkeeper's wife that year, is the 8-year-old with bangs cut straight across her forehead. She kneels in the first row. She holds a lantern up above her hair. I was born in 1954, and my sister, my dear one, died in 1995. I'd never seen this photograph, now on my desk, before 2001. It appears in a mustard-yellow book, *The Beautiful Bronx*, by Lloyd Ultan, founder of *The Bronx County Historical Society Journal*. And I would never have seen the book, I'm certain, save for the fact that my friend John Ashbery sent it to me out of the blue. The pageant cannot remember itself, and then it does. John could not have known that, hidden way in the tall pages, would be a Roberta I'd never seen, exactly as I'd never seen her, really, time out of mind. The affirmation of images has a mind of its own. And you can almost hear the late trains passing by. Transit, not transitive, memory goes ahead of itself and us. Recollection antedates the image whose image is prophetic: in Amor, in Pageant. I never sought to tell my love. Love told Me.

Dove sta memoria...where memory lives and has its being, its Entity. Paradise in transit, including the Interborough Rapid Transit threading lights through the Christmas midnight air of the beautiful Bronx. Perdita's memory antedates her birth and her youth as a shepherdess in Bohemia. Hermione proves it. Coming to life, stepping down from the cold pedestal and into pageant again, she embodies memory in every direction, moving once more. The way up and the way down from the pedestal: one and the same. A fantastic Bohemia and the actual Sicily: one and the same kingdom, in good time. Beatrice arises from a cloud of flowers, *una nuvola di fiori*. She simply lowers her eyes and sets the date June 8 of the year 1290 into motion forever. Dante's memory, addressed to and *by* Eternity (*Guardaci ben!*) antedates his Vision and toil. Where the downward gaze of Beatrice finds him alone and raises him into his proper name, proving the truth of his book, in that exact, dimensionless point, all directions unite. Memory is entity, never anguish anymore. Reunion follows reunion. Finding my sister as innkeeper's wife in a sudden book, exactly as I'd never seen her, six years before I was born and six years after she had died, my pageant remembers itself. The Bronx is beautiful. Long before I was ever a shepherd or a Balthazar, and long afterwards, memory lives there.

OUR NEIGHBORHOOD was an ethnic jumble and, given the turbulence of the 1960s, calm. I'm tempted to say "pastoral," but you wouldn't believe me. Still, with the meadows of Pelham Bay Park to northward, the waters of Long Island Sound to the south, and a blur of City Island east in the sunrise, it was pastoral to many and to me. By 1965, I'd been a shepherd in St. Peter's annual pageant two or three times already, with a golden crown in sight. My new school, Henry Bruckner Junior High, mirrored the neighborhood perfectly in every way; yet with the teachers counted in, numbers began to favor our Italian-American friends. I knew nothing, walking through the gates on the first school day, of Virgil, *Firenze*, and the Papacy, but that was soon to change. I hope you'll believe me. In English class, towards the end of the 45-minute hour, we met a visitor. Miss Petrusa was a small woman

49

with closely cropped coppery-colored hair. She seemed, during the teacher's introduction, literally to vibrate with excitement, although she stood stock still. We learned that our class had been uniquely honored. Beginning Friday, and continuing every Friday for the next three years we would study, instead of ordinary English, *Dante* with Miss Petrusa in the school's small, sunny library: seventh grade, *Inferno*; eighth grade, *Purgatorio*; *Paradiso* in our senior year.

Knowing nothing of Dante, we saw nothing extraordinary or bizarre in the *Commedia*'s displacing *Treasure Island*, *Warriner's Grammar*, and business-letter-writing one day out of every five. We liked the looks of the library; it had tall windows, clean tables, and smelled like Christmas cellophane. Miss Petrusa was always delighted to see us. Never once in our three years, precisely one hundred Fridays, did she become angry or severe. We quickly cherished her. To some of us, she was a doting auntie; to some, myself among them, she was an orphaned gaudy bird. What seemed familiar, we loved. What seemed strange, we intended to protect at all costs from all outsiders.

THE UNGAINLY PAGEANT of our damnation, purgation and bliss went very well. The ceremonies of innocence never drowned, not even among simonists and suicides. The worst that ever happened was that, occasionally, early arrivals would crowd around the illustrated dictionary, parsing genitalia. Miss Petrusa gave no homework. All she asked was that, should an image from the given week's canto catch fire in our minds, we try to capture it with crayons and colored pencils. "Images, images, images" she would exclaim. It was from Miss Petrusa, surely, that I learned to honor the Affirmative Way. To this day, I can draw nothing better than stick-figures in red fires or big roses. But heart and mind, I've entrusted my salvation to Imagery. I've never met an allegory I didn't like. Even in times of imageless darkness and confusion, the sounds of words lead on to kindly light.

Per te poeta fui, per te Cristiano
(*Purgatorio* XX 73)

Given one hundred Fridays and a happy teacher, I've been familiar with eternity quite some time.

IN MAY OF 1967, New Critics ruled the earth, and our class was nearing the end of *Purgatorio*. Accustomed week by week to very close reading and to the vast interiors of our poet's images (Dante was *our* poet by then, and the city of Florence a Bronx with funny little bridges), we'd come to the cantos of Earthly Paradise, to the rivers Lethe and Eunoe, and to new trees at Heaven's brink. It was time for a field trip. On Friday, May 19 we boarded a bus and crossed the river to Manhattan and Fort Tryon Park. Miss Petrusa was taking us to The Cloisters, John D. Rockefeller's anthology of medieval stone and gardens staring down the Palisades. I'd never been to the place; none of us had, though crossing the George Washington Bridge en route to the discount houses of New Jersey, we might have seen it—a blind church on a rocky outcrop. In the years ahead, I'd often spend my birthdays there. In June 1970, in the cloister called Trie, I wrote my earliest poems. But I'm thinking of the very first visit now. More than the altarpieces, tombs and tapestries, more than the unicorns and the fruit trees trained to look like candles, what caught my eye was a single wooden bead.

NETHERLANDISH, scarcely two inches wide, opened to the viewer on a hinge, it is not so much carved *out* of boxwood as *into* it. Look ever so closely, and there's far to go. The eye finds, north and south, two concave hemispheres. To the north is every detail of Christ's nativity—birth and adoration and the flight into Egypt in depth, in intricate relief. The north is Alpha. The south is all Calvary—unimaginable death agony cut in, and cut farther in. Interiors multiply without a vanishing point. The south is Omega. The whole span of Christ's mortality lies open to view. Then the mind remembers what the eye has seen. Here is a single bead. Close it shut upon its hinge; the Alpha and Omega reunite.

51

Mortality floats in an ocean of limitless space and time, a bubble of boxwood, a bead, just one of many of a scattered strand.

HAVING TAUGHT US to read closely on Dante's epic scale, Miss Petrusa, on the 19th day of May 1967 taught us to read an image *alter idem*, inwards, and then farther in. It would be impossible to carve or to pray an entire rosary of such beads. Each is a lifetime self-contained. Alpha prior to Alpha, and Omega after the end merely describe a round surface of boxwood. It is a bubble for bursting, like the sun, never seen to burst. The bead snaps shut. Invisible now to one another, creator and creature are one, and one Love. Subject and object, one and the same. Lover and beloved, one and the same. The entire strand must be the span of lifetimes, dimensionless and without end. A pageant cannot read itself, and then it nearly does. It reunites with all the pageants ongoing. Identity trumps awareness. Beatrice looks down from the visionary car and says to Dante *"Fratre,"* which is to say "Brother." I find my sister gone ahead of me, backwards into a book. I see where she has gone, whenever I wish, in the days remaining. Memory is entity. There is a grain of sand in Lambeth that Satan cannot find.

OUR TIME WITH MISS PETRUSA ended one year later. The last of our Fridays was devoted to *Paradiso*, Canto XXXIII, the finale and periphrasis in Empyrean, a hymn beginning

> *Vergine Madre, figlia del tuo figlio*

The phrase itself is a bead of boxwood. The Virgin Mother, daughter of her only son, perfects in detail, in every mortal and divine specific, Alpha prior to Alpha and Omega without end. Our mothers and fathers, along with school administrators from all around The Bronx, were invited to join us for this last meeting. Miss Petrusa planned something special. We'd be dressed in white as best we could: white shirts and blouses, white chinos and pleated skirts, white sneakers. Gathered choir-fashion, facing our guests, and with our backs to the sunny windows, we'd recite the entire canto, from memory. Then we'd exit, in pageant, past the statuette of Dante by the door.

IT WENT WELL. No one afterwards remembered anything amiss. As for myself, I remember only whiteness, and then walking off. In adult life, reading that final canto again—many, many times—I come to line 64:

Cosi la neve al sol si disigilla

LIKE AN ETERNITY opened upon its hinge, revealing infinite distances, white snow *unsealed (disigilla)* in the sunlight shows a whiteness without end, the chromatic Union directly before and directly after Dante's prismatic word. Here is a credible forecast of Hart Crane's final sky. Here, a "tall decorum" *unseals* earth, showing no gaps. And still it shows every prophecy and soul between my Florentine and my Bedlamite. Man and boy, I have seen it. Passing by the statuette at the door, I *must* have seen.

> Well, I graduated, so you'll have to.
> (John Ashbery, "Gorboduc")

Schooled by overwhelming words and loves—*figlia del tuo figlio*, my older sister younger than myself in ageless pageant, boxwood, boxwood—I read as closely as I can. Reading should be heroic (Thoreau). Where the point of reading loses dimension, I love. We love. Because of the conjugations, it's nothing personal (Eliot). It's prophecy and every soul in between. Every word has a hinge and every footstep a horizon. For Heaven's sake, these are spiritual entities not structural doodads. Structuralists do not exist. Trailing clouds of glory, existence streams the illustrious transactions. Beatrice, smiling for the last time into mortal eyes, your eyes belong to God, where Dante finds them: *e quella…sorrise e riguardommi.* Open a word, Oothoon, and exactly there does knowledge remember itself virginal, unhurt. Hearing footsteps, Perdita, hear the eternal happy shouts of reunion. Little boy in Paumanok, the

outsetting bard should outset *in*. Every word is a ceremony, and
every footstep redoubles the horizon of its home. In the forecourt
of the Temple of Apollo at Delphi, the inscription reads *gnothi
seuton*, "know thyself." Inscribed upon a forecourt, it means "go
in." At this point, alphabets bend. Hemispheres close, one upon
another, death agony upon Christmas adoration, and the rounded
universe is a single bead and the numberless Heaven. If this is
boxwood, it is driving me wild (Jack Spicer).

POEMS ARE WILD FOR PROPHECY, for the quick parlay
of vision into reality. Begun ahead of time, visions move more ways
than one, yet each way is the pattern of itself and cannot change. If
not for the leopard, the lion, and the she-wolf, Dante might have
taken the shortcut. Happily, Virgil takes him in hand, and together
they go the right way round. In visionary transit, knowledge may
hope to find its path to self-knowledge, but only when its vision is
unsealed. How so? In "Years of Indiscretion," John Ashbery offers
a beautiful phrase, *sotto voce*, but in earnest: "vision in the form of a
task." What is the task? To read closely into our loves, remembering
each its place in the pageant. Memory unseals a poet's vision of
these, placing the poet in right relation, and then the pageant
moves. The movement is Prophecy. "Do this in remembrance of
me." Christ's imperative, while spoken quietly, tenderly to friends, is
epical. They have had their Vision: multifoliate nature has affirmed
the images of their inward minds, one and by one. Which is to
say that they know and that they love. Now, Christ calls them to a
task. Knowledge must go beyond the pagan forecourts, into self-
knowledge: *I* love, and I have a name which the Vision speaks to
me, to be written down only then and only by *me*. Love itself must
also move; *l'antica fiamma* must be lifted and carried high, in visible
pageant, along the arc of its homing. Again and again, my poets
redouble the use of memory. It is pure theater, with the emphasis
on "pure," as Perdita, Oothoon, and all the voluptuary star-turns of
poetry sing. The pageant remembers itself a shepherd and a king.

Select Bibliography

John Ashbery. *Some Trees*. New Haven: Yale University Press, 1956.
_____. *The Double Dream of Spring*. New York: Dutton, 1970.
_____. *April Galleons*. New York: Viking, 1987.
W.H. Auden. *The Dyer's Hand*. New York: Random House, 1968.
_____. *Collected Shorter Poems*. New York: Random House, 1975.
Saint Augustine. *Confessions* (trans. R.S. Pine-Coffin). London: Penguin, 1961.
Hart Crane. *The Complete Poems and Selected Letters and Prose* (ed. Brom Weber). New York: Anchor Books, 1966.
Robert Creeley. *The Collected Poems of Robert Creeley 1945-1975*. Berkeley: University of California Press, 1982.
T.S. Eliot. *The Complete Poems and Plays, 1909-1950*. New York: Harcourt, Brace & World, 1962.
_____. *The Selected Prose of T.S. Eliot* (ed. Frank Kermode). New York: Harcourt Brace Jovanovich/Farrar, Straus & Giroux, 1975.
Helen Gardner. *The Art of T.S. Eliot*. London: Faber & Faber, 1949.
C.S. Lewis. *The Allegory of Love*. Cambridge: Cambridge University Press, 1936.
Guillaume de Lorris & Jean de Meun. *The Romance of the Rose* (trans. Harry W. Robbins). New York: Dutton, 1962.
Robert Lowell. *Selected Poems*. New York: Farrar, Straus & Giroux, 2006.
Charles Olson & Robert Creeley. *The Complete Correspondence: Volume 7* (ed. George F. Butterick). Santa Rosa, CA: Black Sparrow, 1987.
Ezra Pound. *The Cantos of Ezra Pound*. New York: New Directions, 1972.
Charles Williams. *The Figure of Beatrice*. Berkeley: The Apocryphile Press, 2005.

Donald Revell is Professor of English at the University of Nevada-Las Vegas. Winner of the PEN USA Translation Award for his translation of Rimbaud's *A Season in Hell* and two-time winner of the PEN USA Award for Poetry, he has also won the Academy of American Poets Lenore Marshall Prize and is a former fellow of the Ingram Merrill and Guggenheim Foundations. Additionally, he has twice been granted fellowships in poetry from the National Endowment for the Arts. Former editor-in-chief of Denver Quarterly, he now serves as poetry editor of Colorado Review. Revell lives in the desert south of Las Vegas with his wife, poet Claudia Keelan, and their children, Benjamin Brecht and Lucie Ming.

Essay: A Critical Memoir by Donald Revell

Cover Art: *Beatrice Addressing Dante from the Car*
from *Illustrations to Dante's 'Divine Comedy'*, 1824–27
Pen and ink and watercolor on paper. Dimensions 372 x 527 mm.
Artist: William Blake, 1757–1827, © Tate, London

Cover typeface: Kabel LT Std.
Interior Typefaces: Trajan Pro and Adobe Jenson Pro

Book cover and interior design by Ken Keegan

Each Omnidawn author participates fully in the design of his or her
book, choosing cover art and approving cover and interior design.
Omnidawn strives to create books that align with each author's vision.

Offset printed in the United States
by Edwards Brothers Malloy, Ann Arbor, Michigan
On 55# Heritage Book Cream
Acid Free Archival Quality Recycled Paper
with Rainbow FSC Certified Colored End Papers

Publication of this book was made possible in part by gifts from:
Robin & Curt Caton
Deborah Klang Smith

Omnidawn Publishing
Richmond, California
2015
Rusty Morrison & Ken Keegan, Senior Editors & Publishers
Gillian Olivia Blythe Hamel, Managing Editor, Book Designer,
& OmniVerse Managing Editor
Sharon Zetter, Poetry Editor, Grant Writer & Book Designer
Cassandra Smith, Poetry Editor & Book Designer
Peter Burghardt, Poetry Editor & Book Designer
Melissa Burke, Marketing Manager & Poetry Editor
Liza Flum, Poetry Editor & Social Media
Juliana Paslay, Fiction Editor & Bookstore Outreach Manager
Gail Aronson, Fiction Editor
RJ Ingram, Poetry Editor & Social Media
Josie Gallup, Feature Writer
Sheila Sumner, Feature Writer
Kevin Peters, Feature Writer